IMPRIMATUR
+ Most Reverend Robert J. McManus, S.T.D.
Bishop of Worcester
March 10, 2020

TEXT: Anne-Isabelle Lacassagne, translation by Woodeene Koenig-Bricker
Illustrations: Isabelle Monnerot-Dumaine

EDITORIAL: David Dziena, Therese Ratliff
(© Les Petits Brins of Isabelle) www.lespetitsbrins.com, @lespetitsbrinsdisabelle

GRAPHIC DESIGN: Virginie Lafon, Jeff McCall

19, rue de la Saillerie - CS 10002
49184 Saint-Barthélemy-d'Anjou Cedex
www.editions.crer-bayard.fr
Law No. 49-956 of 16 July, 1949 on publications intended for
youth, modified by the law number: 2011-525 of May 17, 2011.

Pflaum Publishing Group
3055 Kettering Blvd., Suite 100
Dayton, OH 45439
800-543-4383
Pflaum.com

ISBN: 978-1-947358-29-4
Printed in China.

bayard A division of Bayard, Inc.

Justin and Mia Discover

THE TREASURES OF THE MASS

Anne-Isabelle Lacassagne · Isabelle Monnerot-Dumaine

On Sunday, Justin and Mia are walking with their parents.

They stop in front of the church and look inside.

"It looks like someone is getting ready for a party," says Justin. "Can we go inside?"

Mom says, "The church is the house of God. We are all invited."

"But what are we invited to?" asks Mia.

"To go to Mass," says Dad.

"We went to Mass last Christmas," Justin recalls.

"So, should we go again?" Mom offers.

FOR PARENTS

The church is the house of God, but it's also our home. We can go there whenever we want. We can walk around inside, sit quietly, pray with our children or sing with them, light a candle... Most importantly, we go to church each Sunday (or Saturday evening) to attend Mass.

When Justin and Mia come in, a tall man dressed in a green and white robe smiles at them. He is the parish priest, Father Martin.

Mia asks him, "Is Mass for children?"

"Yes, of course," Father Martin says.

"But what are we going to do at Mass?" asks Mia.

Father Martin answers, "Mass is like a treasure hunt."

"What are we looking for?" asks Justin, who is very interested.

"The special treasures that God wants to share with us," Father Martin says.

FOR PARENTS

What do we see when we enter the church? Walk down the main aisle that leads to the altar. Around the church there may be statues and paintings. What do we feel when we enter? What do we experience? What touches us?

Justin and Mia sit next to Simon the catechist. Today he is helping the children to participate in the Mass.

"So, this treasure hunt," Mia asks him. "When does it start?"

"Do you hear the music?" Simon asks. "We begin the Mass by singing all together."

"Like we're all on the same team," Justin says.

"Or part of the same family," adds Mia.

"This family is the family of those who are baptized," explains Simon.

FOR PARENTS

All of us are part of the big family of those who are baptized. God knows each of our names. We can stop by the baptismal font to tell our children about the day they were baptized.

While everyone is singing, a procession begins moving toward the sanctuary and altar.

Mia asks, “Why is Father Martin walking behind a great big cross?”

“The cross is the sign of the friends of Jesus,” Justin recalls.

“We come together to meet Jesus,” says Dad.

FOR PARENTS

There may be many crosses in a church. We can first search for them and count them together to make sure that children understand the importance of this sign before we explain it.

Everyone says, "In the name of the Father, the Son and the Holy Spirit. Amen."

Justin remembers what his grandmother told him: "The Father is God because he loves us as his children."

"The Son of God is Jesus," says Mia. "But what is the Holy Spirit?"

"That's more difficult to explain," Simon says. "The Holy Spirit is the power of God. The Spirit is like the wind that pushes us forward and gives us God's special help."

"And what does 'Amen' mean?" Mia continues.

"'Amen' is our response," says Dad. "It is like saying a very strong 'Yes! I believe!'"

FOR PARENTS

To make the Sign of the Cross, begin by touching the forehead (1), saying, "In the name of the Father." Then touch the center of the chest (2) and say, "And of the Son." Next, touch the left shoulder (3) saying, "Holy." Conclude with the right shoulder (4) by saying, "Spirit. Amen."

Simon asks, "What do you wear when you are invited to a party?"

"My best dress," says Mia.

Simon smiles and goes on. "When we enter the house of God, we try to look good on the outside, but sometimes we feel different on the inside. We know we didn't do our best and could have done better. Our sins are like a stain on our clothes. That's why at the beginning of the Mass, we ask God to forgive us."

FOR PARENTS

What is sin?
It's doing something on purpose that we know is wrong. Sin can hurt those around us and it makes us unhappy, too. But God loves us and wants us to be happy, filled with love for everyone.

"Glory to God in the highest!" proclaims the assembly.

"We sing about our joy," says Mom. "God loves us. When we seek God, God forgives us and welcomes us as an all-loving Father whose love is never ending!"

"Glory to God!' sing Justin and Mia with all the assembly.

FOR PARENTS

To praise God is to see things differently, to marvel, to seek the traces of God in our lives. We thank God for all the good things in our world!

Everyone sits down.

"Listen carefully!" says Dad. "Don't forget that we are looking for a treasure."

Simon explains, "We listen to the Word of God in the Bible. This book tells the story of a certain people called the Hebrews. God told them, 'I love you. I will be like a father to you.' And the Hebrews answered, 'We love you, God.' The Bible is the story of this extraordinary relationship between God and humanity."

FOR PARENTS

The Bible is like a library of books, each more thrilling than the next. We can tell our children some of these stories or read from a children's Bible. We can also choose to read the Bible itself without explaining everything. That way we let the story of God's Word transport us.

Now everyone sings together!

"It's the Responsorial Psalm. Psalms are a kind of song," explains Simon. "The ancient psalms passed on from generation to generation, from the Hebrew people to us. We pray the very same prayers!"

"Prayer to God never stops," says Dad.

"That may be the treasure," Justin whispers to Mia.

FOR PARENTS

The psalms often begin with a cry, sometimes of joy, fear, or pain. As a family, when you go through difficulties, you can entrust your problems to God with the help of the Psalms. We can even ask God, "What are you doing, Lord? Come to my aid!"

Simon explains, "Now, we're going to listen to a second reading from the Bible. It is chosen from special writings by the first followers of Jesus. They traveled far and wide to announce the Good News to the whole world."

"What Good News?" wonders Mia.

Mom answers, "They had met someone extraordinary."

"It's Jesus," Justin guesses.

FOR PARENTS

Talking about the Apostles can provide an opportunity to learn how they are represented in the Church. For example, Saint Peter holds keys, indicating he holds the keys to Heaven; Saint Paul is shown with a sword at his side, reminding us of his death by beheading.

Everyone stands up and sings, "Alleluia!" It is a cry of joy. Praise be the Lord!

FOR PARENTS
Before the Proclamation of the Gospel, we make a small cross on our forehead, lips, and heart. We think silently, "May the Gospel be on my mind, on my lips, and in my heart" as we touch each place. At the same time, we say aloud, "Glory to you, O Lord."

Simon explains, "The priest is now reading about events in the life of Jesus from a special section of the Bible called the Gospels. Along with his disciples, Jesus traveled far and wide to meet people. On the road, he stopped to listen, help, and sometimes even heal. Jesus told them that even the least among us are loved by God with immense love."

Justin whispers to his sister, "Do you think that the treasure of God is love?"

Everyone sits down.

Father Martin says, "Because of what he preached, Jesus was arrested and sentenced to death on a cross. Even though his followers believed that everything was over, three days after his death, Jesus had risen!"

"What does 'risen' mean?" Mia asks.

"He was alive again," Mom answers.

Simon adds, "That's why the Sign of the Cross is so important. It's a sign of victory. God's love is stronger than anything."

"And the treasure? Is it the strong love of God?" asks Justin.

FOR PARENTS

What do we do when our children have trouble following the homily? We can suggest that each of us listen for one idea or one word that we will then share at home with the rest of the family as a treasure.

Everyone stands to recite a prayer.

Simon explains, "We believe that the Good News we have heard is true. Jesus Christ is alive today. That's why we say the the Creed, which means 'I believe.'"

FOR PARENTS

The word *credo* comes from Latin *credere* which means "I believe." By reciting the Creed, we renew our faith and are reminded of everything the Christian community believes, and we are connected to all Christians who have gone before us.

Someone speaks into a microphone, saying, "Lord, we entrust to you all those who suffer."

Dad remarks, "When we pray, we, too, entrust those who are unhappy to God."

"Why?" Mia asks.

Mom answers, "We believe that God hears our prayers and always responds to them."

"How does God do that?" asks Justin.

Dad explains, "God acts in the world. We are the messengers of God's love. We can smile and help those we meet on our way."

FOR PARENTS

What is beautiful about this prayer is that we are all praying together for the needs of the world. Throughout the whole world, there are people who are praying. Prayer is an invisible force, a surge of love that expands throughout the world.

With Simon, Justin and Mia move from pew to pew.
They carry baskets that they offer to everyone present.
People place money in the basket.

"Is this paying for Mass?" Justin asks.

"No," Simon answers. "The money collected is a gift to help the Church do good things in the world. People give whatever they can."

In procession, Justin and Mia bring up the offering baskets.

Alongside the offering baskets, bread and wine are also brought up to the altar.

"A meal is being prepared," says Mia happily.

FOR PARENTS

What is the purpose of the offering? Our Church is an community that cares for each other. The offering is used to help the Church with its needs, but also to help those who are less fortunate than we are.

Father Martin holds up the host and says, "Blessed are you, Lord God of all creation, for through your goodness we have received the bread we offer you: fruit of the earth and work of human hands, it will become for us the bread of life."

Justin whispers, "What does 'bread of life' mean?"

"God is doing something very precious with this bread," answers Simon.

"Another treasure?" Mia asks.

FOR PARENTS

Host **is the name that we give to the bread used during Mass. It is unleavened, like the unleavened bread of the Hebrews.**

Father Martin prays with his hands raised.

"This prayer," explains Simon, "is different during different times of the year because we go from one holy day to the next. Do you know some?"

"Christmas," answers Mia.

"Easter," adds Justin.

"The vestment of the priest changes color according to the time of year," explains Dad. "It can be green, red, purple, or white."

FOR PARENTS

GREEN
For growing, the color of Ordinary Time

RED
For love and sacrifice, the color of Palm Sunday and Good Friday

PURPLE
For waiting and penance, the color of Advent and Lent

WHITE
For celebration, the color of Christmas and Easter

Simon explains, "Father Martin will now say the words Jesus spoke during his last meal. We are invited to relive that moment together."

The priest takes the host and says, "At the time he was betrayed and entered willingly into his Passion, he took bread and, giving thanks, broke it, and gave it to his disciples, saying: 'Take this, all of you, and eat of it: for this is my body which will be given up for you.'"

Everyone bows their heads in respect.

Slowly Simon explains, "That day Jesus gave himself completely. He is the bread of life."

FOR PARENTS

While kneeling, remain attentive during the Consecration. Even small children can recognize this moment as special.

FOR PARENTS

Jesus is present for us at each Mass, in the consecrated bread and wine which have become the Body and Blood of Christ. It is difficult to understand. But it's what we believe, and it's wonderful to know that Jesus is truly present with us in this way.

Father Martin takes the chalice and says, “In a similar way, when supper was ended, he took the chalice and, once more giving thanks, he gave it to his disciples, saying: ‘Take this, all of you, and drink from it: for this is the chalice of my blood, the blood of the new and eternal covenant, which will be poured out for you and for many for the forgiveness of sins. Do this in memory of me.’”

Everyone bows their heads in respect.

"Jesus taught us a prayer," Simon says. "Do you know it?"

"The Our Father," says Justin, proud that he remembers.

All say:

Our Father who art in heaven,
Hallowed be thy name,
Thy kingdom come,
Thy will be done on earth as it is in heaven.
Give us this day our daily bread.
And forgive us our trespasses,
as we forgive those
who trespass against us.
And lead us not into temptation
but deliver us from evil. Amen

FOR PARENTS

There are two parts of the Our Father: a prayer of praise, then a prayer of request. Praying together with our children is a very special moment. First, we praise God for the many blessings we have received, then we simply ask for what we need.

Simon explains, "Jesus gives us another gift. He offers us his peace." Then he adds, "This peace is given to us by the priest in the name of Jesus. We pass this peace from person to person throughout our church. In this way, we, too, bring this peace to those around us."

"The peace of Christ," say Justin and Mia, turning to their parents.

FOR PARENTS

When we give a sign of peace, it is recognizing that we are brothers and sisters in the same family—the family of the baptized who follow Christ.

Justin and Mia watch the people approaching the sanctuary.

"They are going to receive Communion," explains Simon.

"I want to receive the host, too," says Mia.

"Right now you cannot," Simon answers, "because you have not made your First Communion. You must wait and make the first time you receive Communion into a celebration."

"As if we are receiving a treasure," says Justin, who understands.

Justin and Mia walk toward the altar with their arms folded in front of them.

Father Martin traces a cross on Mia's forehead.
He says, "Christ be with you."

FOR PARENTS

What do you say to a child who wants to receive Communion but hasn't made their First Communion? It's an opportunity to explain how special the Eucharist is and to help them eagerly look forward to their First Communion by learning more about the life of Jesus and his friends.

FOR PARENTS

To bless is to ask God that goodness comes to a person. This action is not restricted to a priest. We can bless our children. It is a way to tell them that God is there with them and loves them.

Father Martin says, "May almighty God bless you, the Father, and the Son, and the Holy Spirit."

Justin and Mia make the Sign of the Cross and answer, "Amen."

"By this blessing, God makes us a promise," explains Simon. "His love stays with us all throughout the week."

"So, it's not over?" asks Justin.

"No," Dad answers. "This is just the beginning."

FOR PARENTS

Sunday, for Christians, is not the last day of the week. It is the first! We become bearers of the treasures of the Mass. It is up to us to take what we have received out into the world.

In the vestibule, Father Martin talks with Justin, Mia, and their parents. "So, did you find the treasures of God?"

"Yes," answer the children. "God gives us a special gift of love!"

"By speaking to us in the Word," says Justin.

"By feeding us with the bread and the wine that are Jesus' Body and Blood," continues Mia.

Their parents add, "By gathering with the whole community."

"And by being sent into the world to spread the Good News of Jesus," concludes Father Martin.

Around them, people come forward to talk to them.

"I feel like we're going to make lots of new friends," Justin says.

"And we'll come back because the house of God is our house, too," replies Mia.

FOR PARENTS

The treasures of the Mass continue in the vestibule (church entrance). Take the time to welcome and be welcomed, to feel the warmth of a community, and to help the children feel at home.

During the Mass, like Justin and Mia, we seek the treasures that God wants to share with us. We join the great family of Christians and pray together. Then we listen to the Word of God and let it resonate in us. We are invited to share a holy meal with Jesus. Finally, we leave with our hearts filled with all these treasures and go to spread the joy of God's love to all we meet! Thank you, Lord!

Introductory Rites

Liturgy of the Word

Liturgy of the Eucharist

Communion Rite

Concluding Rite